December 2013

The NGOS and the new mechanisms for funds mobilization

Action Research

"The NGOS and the new mechanisms for funds mobilization"

Hicham ABDEDINE

Special thanks to *Wiam ABDEDINE* and *Imane ABDEDINE*, for translating this book from its original language (French) to English.

SUMMARY

This research is a look at the basics of fundraising for Solidarity International Organizations and national. This is an action research which puts light on the role and approach fundraising for to maintain their existence and sustain their field actions. Thus, this document provides essential elements to make NGOs effective fundraising, sustainable and relevant...

The charitable works or even charities which are also non-profit develop projects of public interest. To be able to ensure their long-term mission, these organizations are located in the need for regular financial resources.

These recent come from various sources: governments, foundations, businesses or individuals. The English expression "Fundraising » or lifting of funds is used widely on the international plane. "Fundraising" means bringing together of capital. In the charitable associations, we speak rather of collection of donations. It is simply to develop a strategy for effective communication in order to provide the necessary financial means.

1) The tools of the Fundraising

There are various ways to collect funds and retain the generous donors. The image and the presentation of your organization as well as the relationship coming from the custom dialog, play a crucial role for weaving a relational link with donors.

There are several ways to collect donations:

Among the conventional means, include the sending of a mail or mailing, the collection of donations in public places, the direct contact by phone, the sponsorships, the testamentary bequests, the donations granted by enterprises, the state subsidies, financing through cantonal fund of the Lottery Romande, cultural or sporting events, the sale of various products, the donations through the Internet or by SMS text messages. Many sources of funding are possible. These sources can ensure the financing of NGOS when they are well utilized.

2) The logic of the Donation

We mean by a donation, the payment of a sum of money in favor of a human cause without waiting for a counterpart.

To perform regular donations, donors must be convinced by the validity of the association that they support. For this, it is essential to keep the donor regularly informed about the projects of the organization of its activities and more particularly its achieved results. The monitoring of the most generous donors is very important. This work requires a lot of attention and human resources, an extensive correspondence and a personal relationship followed during many years, the sending of letters of thanks from journals outlining the achievements. The obtaining of large donations need a sustainable relationship and respect to the generous donors.

3) The Sponsoring and Sponsorship

The sponsoring is differentiated from sponsorship, because it involves the benefits granted in return. The company sponsor in return requires a certain degree of visibility (mention of the logo of the company) in the media of communication, here it is a hidden advertising behind the human values or even that the company acquires the SER (Social and Environmental Responsibility).

Thus, by the commitments of sponsorship, the company aims to increase or improve its capital sympathy and consolidate its brand image with its customers or partners.

4) The public relations

The public relations are used to enhance the image of the organization to the general public. The outcome of fundraising activities depends closely on public relations and the image that the organization will be able to give of itself.

5) Sustaining the relationship with donors

The donation in question is not sufficient. It is essential to establish an exclusive and lasting relationship between the organization and the donors so as to ensure the permanence of the funds as well as the survival of the humanitarian action.

The success of a fundraising strategy of quality depends mainly on the personal relations that the leadership of an organization can weave with donors. In effect, creating certain complicity between generous donors and officials of an organization allows you to establish strong and lasting relationships.

The most important thing is to establish close relations with the regular donors, as well as those who pay substantial donations. The donors whom we trust are showing generally more generous. In the light of our experience, the most generous donations come from 20 per cent of regular donors.

6) The custom speech

The custom speech represents the best way to convince the potential donors. In the context of a telephone campaign, the likelihood of obtaining a donation increases when the interlocutors actually know each other. The person who contacts the donor should manage the situation by following a strict scenario and be able to react accordingly. This requires a lot of tact, especially when it comes to learning about the possible amount that the donor would be willing to pay.

7) How does the fundraising work by phone?

The dialog by phone is one of the most effective ways to motivate a person to make a donation in favor of a charitable association. The phone call brings people together because the conversation allows you to understand and quickly assess the state of mind of the interlocutors. The transmission of information concerning the organization is facilitated. As well, potential donors will be quicker *to* access the queries of the organization.

The fundraising by phone offers many advantages: thanks to the direct relationship that allows verbal communication, it is easier to introduce and clarify the projects, as well as the objectives of the organization. In addition, the telephone interview is the best way to know the opinion of people and answer any questions.

The preparation of a campaign phone requires the prior development of a detailed protocol of the content of telephone conversations. This allows you to anticipate the favorable responses to a donation, the compliments or any criticism and to react more quickly to the questions of the donors.

8)   The benefits of fundraising by phone

20 Years of experience in this field we show that the communication by phone has lost nothing of its attractiveness. Since the phone reveals the whole subtle palette and the richness of human relations and allows a flexibility and creativity almost limitless.

9)   Variety of methods

The Fundraising by phone is ideal when one has the following objectives:

- Automatic sampling of donations on a bank account authorized,

- Retention of the donor,

- Reactivation of inactive donors,

- Refresh the coordinates of the actual or prospective donors,

- Express gratitude to the people who have paid large sums,

- Strengthen the impact when it is question of proposing a sponsorship.

Even during a campaign of acquisition of new donors, the phone is really effective. A quick telephone survey will unveil the turning that will take a campaign. If the organization wishes to make a few changes to the scenario, they can be applied immediately. In the case where the campaign does not encounter the success expected, it is also possible to renounce the telephone interviews. Our guarantee of deficit keeps you safe from any risk of unnecessary spending.

10) Professional planning as a key to success

The Fundraising includes very specific characteristics of the acquisition system at different levels. The largest share of the charitable associations develops and organizes the different steps necessary to ensure the success of the telephone campaign.

- *The distribution/provision of tasks* : Here are the elements that guarantee a good preparation: sending a letter prior to the beginning of the telephone campaign, drafting the script, studying thoroughly the most frequently asked questions by the donors, searching for phone numbers, test phases, preselecting addresses, data base management, comparative administration of addresses, briefing of telephone operators and collaborators of the client's organization, and finally confirming the campaign/conditions of the contract.

-   *The Calls:* We are paying a special attention to the coordination, the quality and the outcome of the telephone calls, also to the motivation of our employees, to the adequacy of the scripts as well as the statistics of the results of the calls.

-   *The follow up:* We attach a particular care to the drafting style of the mail; we add to it demands for clarification and convey our remarks or possible questions. Finally, we count the addresses and write the final reports.

-   *The acquisition of donors* via the phone calls however requires a certain investment to be profitable. The telephone operators are aware that a donation depends on the quality of a conversation. Sometimes a prolonged conversation is necessary for a positive conclusion from a telephone call. The impact of a telephone call counts a lot to retain donors. The emotion created in the course of the conversation is essential in the deed for the donation.

11)   Increase the donations of your donors

There is nothing more rewarding than a successful telephone conversation leading to obtaining a donation from the faithful donors. The persons contacted are delighted to communicate with the organization that they support and have a sense of recognition and gratitude towards. Often, these donors willingly pay a regular sum to their association by making use of the direct bank recovery or the flow of the post. This system therefore enjoys a favorable reception among the faithful donors.

12) The success lies in the similar links to friendship

Obtaining a promise of donations from your donors is not an easy thing. In effect, these delicate relations require particular attention encompassing of the instruments of marketing such as letters of appreciation, invitations to events, written reports on the campaigns, and, periodically, telephone contacts. An intelligent and followed approach by this segment of donors allows to win a greater customers' loyalty and to promote donations from them. The number of donations from donors linked to an organization is estimated to be 70%.

13) Reactivation of inactive donors

The secret of marketing in the sector of donations lies in a correct management of the files of addresses of regular donors. By their donations, the latter have demonstrated their interest in an organization and their willingness to support its projects. The sending of one or two letters refers to reviving their solicitude and providing current information on the organization. This approach also generates donations. We find that among the contacts of a database, some of them are no longer donating since 18 to 36 months. It is this sector that should be managed better because these people have demonstrated in the past a certain interest. It would be a shame to lose them. Therefore how can we retrieve these former donors?

14) The Fundraising through the phone

Our experience demonstrates that resuming the dialog by phone is effective since 80% of donors can be contacted by telephone. During the telephone dialog, the causes of refusal are quickly established and the misunderstandings are excluded. About 60% of people contacted by phone request a renewal of donations. In addition, persons whom weren't possibly contacted, or those who absolutely refused, represent 50% of the removed contacts from the list. This sort of addresses allows you to delete any unnecessary investment in the inactive contacts. On the contrary, the dialog can be resumed with the other contacts. Statistics show that 55% to 65% of them are ready to renew their membership status.

The net revenues of a campaign to collect donations by telephone from donor and non-donor assets are by force less important things than those obtained by appealing to the assets on this day -however, even this segment may seem interesting!

15) Targeted research of new donors

Each charitable association has experienced the decrease of faithful donors. In addressing this question, it can be seen that the causes are various: death, relocation, disinterest, etc. to acquire new donors, it is necessary to communicate with young generations, which will become the future donors, and try to win their support.

16) Best practices and advice to NGOs to collect donations online

- *Choose collecting donations provider that embraces Web 2.0*

From PayPal to Google Checkout, through JustGive and Netwo rkforGood across aiderenligne or aiderdonner in France, there is a plethora of providers that can process donations for your organization. Processing fees range from 2.9% to 4.75%. Of all these suppliers, **Network for Good has paved the way for the adoption of**fundraising **Web 2.0 tools.** If someone makes a donation to your organization via Facebook Causes,

Change.org or Razoo, the donation is processed by Network for Good.

• *Place a big and colorful button "Donate" on your page "Support us!"*

Online donors respond well to buttons. A link "Donate Now" is not enough. Your provider will give you a button or if you have a graphic artist, you can create **a** custom button that will connect you directly to your donation page. To see an example, check "I give" on the Red Cross website. Note also the security argument.

• *Add a "Donate" button on every page of your website*

If possible, add a link "Donate" on every page of your website. Médecins du monde has made that choice. We must reduce the risk of change of mind or loss of donor. This link must lead to a page that lists the **many ways for** a future donor to donate to your organization.

- ***The button "Donate" should be connected directly to a web page that asks for contact information and credit card***

When a sympathizer visits your site and clicks on "Donate", the link should **go** directly to the **page where donors enter their contact information and their credit card.** The "Donate" button should never lead a donor to a generic page under pain of disappointing and risk of a donor loss.

- ***Add a "Donate" to your Facebook page***

Using the application <u>Static FBML</u> on **Facebook,** you can add **a tab or "Donation" button on your Facebook page.** With some knowledge of html, you can easily add a "Donation" on your Facebook page that links directly to the page gift of your web site or allowing a donation directly as for the <u>Reporters Without Borders page.</u>

Facebook is not the most appropriate tool for donation but it has the advantage of being very public. You can also create a link to Causes.

• Perfect your "gift" page to make it effective and attractive.

It is necessary to have a "gift" page [Give / Support our work] which includes information **on** the different ways **for a donor to donate.** Stay simple and clear like the page <u>Médecins du monde</u> as an example. Make sure that the "Donate" button has priority over the page.

• Make sure your "gift" page includes a mailing address

Many people continue to issue checks for donations. Yet many NGOs make the mistake, which is non-including a street address on their page "gift". The "contact" page is not sufficient since potential donors may be asked whether this is the right address to make donations.

• Never require a phone number to make a donation online

This requirement diverts many donors online. If you want to ask the donor to subscribe to your list of SMS alerts, offer it as an option or on the gratitude page after the gift, but we must not in any case make the registration of its phone number a requirement. See for example <u>Oxfam.</u>

- **_Highlight the recurring donations and support programs_**

JustGive Network for Good allow donors to schedule **recurring donations** in the amount of their choice. Once signed, many donors continue to give for years. The Humane Society is a good example to encourage the monthly donations. MSF offers 1 per week from its home page and set up a dedicated website.

In addition, many NGOs are launching support programs and showing this on their website, in their newsletter on their blog, their Facebook page and Twitter account. Adhesions in programs develop slowly, especially at first, but can become a constant source of a regular income for your organization.

- **_Offer the opportunity to donate in someone's name_**

Again, JustGive Network for Good and allow donors to **give to someone's name.** This feature is very common in Anglo-Saxon countries, and less in France. It is however very useful especially during the holidays when many prefer to make a donation on behalf of someone rather than buying a new useless gift to 20. This can also be an idea for weddings;

birthdays ... The trick is to highlight this device on your website, newsletter, blog and other online presence points. You will also need **gift** cards to send to recipients. Start small and just buy some nice cards in a paper mill.

- ***Add buttons Facebook, Twitter, YouTube to your thank you page***

After a donor has made a donation online on your site, it usually ends up on a "Thank you for your donation!" page. Make sure that the page **also** has **links to social networks.** Explain that it can **afford** you to stay **informed** about the work of your organization and progress.

On this point, it is clear that social media, to the extent that they allow new opportunities to reach the donor, require the same time to rethink communication on field projects on these social media. That is when all the information production on the projects that must be rethought and reorganized.

- ***The mailing works!***

Remember the **mailing** admittedly little sexy, but it works very well. If the community is active and targeting is accurate, the conversion rate can be very effective. The mailing can be used to highlight emergencies **and** to mobilize quickly. Remember that not everyone is active on social networks.

- ***Explain how funds will be used***

. Transparency encourages donors. So <u>MSF</u> shows how 1   will be used.   <u>Handicap International,</u> for encouraging large donations, highlights what a sum can do: 7   is suf ficient to provide prosthesis to a child, 50   for prosthesis plus rehabilitation,   100 for prosthesis, rehabilitatio n and a school kit. People rescue will even go further to propose <u>to choose the allocation of the donation.</u>

- ***Your supporters gather for you (crowd funding)***

On the web, as in **life,** supporters **are the first spokesmen of associations.** The social web encourages and relies on it. Tweet messages and do retweets. Encourage sharing on Facebook. Create widgets for bloggers or those who have a website. Make supporters even participate in viral campaigns. For example, the Telethon launched in 2007 <u>"This is your heart"</u> with the goal of becoming the longest world viral video. It may also involve those sympathizers in events like the <u>race of heroes</u> by allowing them to take ownership of the event, to collect for the sake of an association and to broadcast the message.

CONCLUSION

The best method for soliciting potential donors is to be present at various events with a booth that outlines and describes the activities of the organization. It is also possible to send mailings to people who are supposed to have an affinity with the organization. However these mailings do not guarantee a very high response rate. In other words, the addresses of which we ignore the reaction are called "cold" addresses. We noticed in these past few years a recession of the results of mailings and a difficulty to find new donors in this saturated market.

The telephone contact reveals his/her effectiveness because he/she allows you to expand the circle of people ready to engage durably toward the organization. Even if the beginning of a campaign is difficult, it is worth persevering for because the quality of the interviews may be very promising afterwards.

BIBLIOGRAPHY

- Marketing and communication of associations, Karine Gallopel-Morvan , Pierre Birambeau, Fabrice Larceneux, Sophie Rieunier, 2nd edition Dunod, 2013, 22 p.

- The marketing of charitable associations, Heloise BARBIER, study franco/german, 2005, 89 p.

- Prospecting postal and telephone, National Commission on Information Technology and Freedoms CNIL, edition March 2014.

- The innovative financing of associations and foundations: State of places and prospects, France generosities, December 2013, 57 p.

- Guide for the collection of funds for the volunteers of the UNITERRA program.